D1717135

TABLE OF CONTENTS

SCORING RUN

It is April 3, 2017. Gonzaga faces North Carolina in the National Collegiate Athletic Association (NCAA) championship game. Gonzaga leads 65–63. There are less than two minutes to go.

Then, North Carolina goes on a roll. Justin Jackson hits a shot. Isaiah Hicks drives to the hoop for a layup. Jackson slam dunks the basketball. North Carolina wins 71–65. They are NCAA champs!

JUSTIN
JACKSON

BASKETBALL CHAMPS

2017 was the sixth time North Carolina won the NCAA championship.

PERKINS
13

WHAT IS THE FINAL FOUR?

"Final Four" is the popular name for the NCAA basketball championship. There is a men's and women's tournament.

The tournament is single-elimination. When teams win, they advance to the next round. Losing teams are removed from the tournament. "Final Four" refers to the last four teams remaining in the tournament.

The NCAA championship is held every year. It is played at the end of the college basketball season. It begins in the middle of March.

There is an incredible amount of excitement surrounding the tournament. Fans call this time of year "March Madness." All across the nation, people cheer on their favorite college teams.

HISTORY OF THE NCAA CHAMPIONSHIP

In 1906, the NCAA was created to oversee the rules of all college sports. The first NCAA men's basketball tournament was held in 1939. There were only eight teams.

In 1946, the final four teams met in one location. Their games were played at Madison Square Garden in New York City. The idea of the Final Four began to take form.

1939
NCAA CHAMPIONSHIP

FINAL FOUR

"Final Four" was first used in 1975 to refer to the NCAA championship.

11

Over the years, the NCAA championship tournament has grown. It expanded to 16 teams in 1951. In 1975, there were 32 teams. Now, there are 68.

The women's first NCAA championship tournament was in 1982. There were only 32 teams. Today, 64 teams qualify.

FINAL FOUR CHAMPS

[MEN]
UCLA

1964, 1965, 1967, 1968,
1969, 1970, 1971, 1972,
1973, 1975, 1995

NCAA MVP ·················▶

Kareem Abdul-Jabbar led
the Bruins to three straight
championships. He also
won many awards.

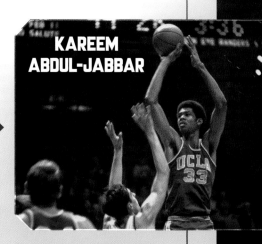

KAREEM
ABDUL-JABBAR

[WOMEN]
UCONN

1995, 2000, 2002, 2003,
2004, 2009, 2010, 2013,
2014, 2015, 2016

NCAA MVP ·················▶

Breanna Stewart helped
the Huskies win four
championships. She
also received the Most
Outstanding Player
award four times.

BREANNA
STEWART

ROAD TO
THE NCAA
CHAMPIONSHIP

Teams get into the NCAA championship tournament in two ways. The winning team from each of the 32 college conference tournaments is added.

FIRST FOUR

The men's tournament starts with the First Four round. In it, 8 teams play for four spots among the top 64 teams.

Then, at-large bids are given to 36 teams. These teams are voted on by a selection committee. Its members review teams' records and games played. They try to pick the best teams for the tournament.

Teams are divided into four regions of 16 teams. When 16 winning teams are left in the tournament, it is called the Sweet Sixteen round. When 8 teams are left, it is the Elite Eight round.

SEEDINGS

Teams in each region are ranked from 1 to 16. The top-ranked teams start by playing the bottom-ranked teams.

The winning team of each region enters the Final Four round. They are paired into semifinal games. These decide who plays for the championship.

NCAA TOURNAMENT BRACKET

SOUTH
REGIONAL

WEST
REGIONAL

FIRST ROUND	SECOND ROUND	REGIONAL SEMIFINALS SWEET SIXTEEN	REGIONAL FINALS ELITE EIGHT	NATIONAL SEMIFINALS FINAL FOUR

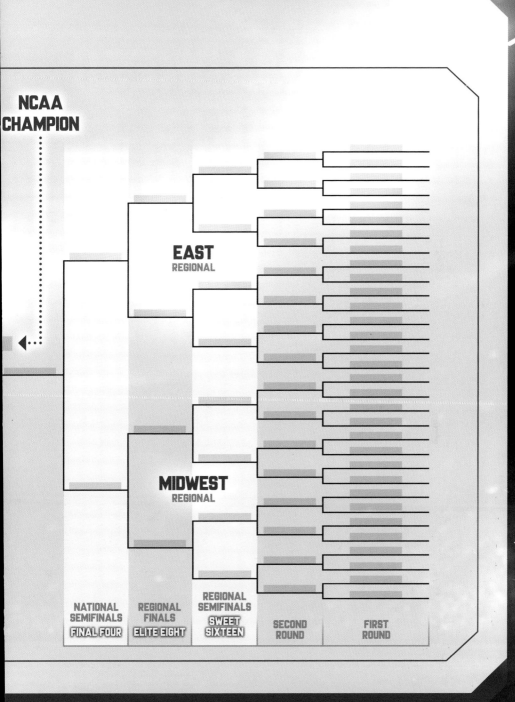

NCAA
CHAMPION

EAST
REGIONAL

MIDWEST
REGIONAL

NATIONAL SEMIFINALS	REGIONAL FINALS	REGIONAL SEMIFINALS	SECOND ROUND	FIRST ROUND
FINAL FOUR	ELITE EIGHT	SWEET SIXTEEN		

MARCH MADNESS BRACKETS

Fans root for their favorite teams during March Madness. They also fill out brackets. People challenge each other to guess the winners of each game during the tournament. The person who picks the most correct games and the champion wins!

Keeping track of a bracket is just one exciting reason to tune in to the NCAA championship tournament!

GLOSSARY

at-large bids—spots in a tournament given to teams by an invitation

brackets—the pairing up of opponents in a tournament

conference—a large grouping of sports teams that often play each other

layup—a shot made near the basket often by bouncing the ball off the backboard

qualify—to earn a spot in a tournament

regions—areas

semifinal—related to the games played right before the final game in a tournament

single-elimination—a type of tournament in which teams no longer play if they lose a game

tournament—a series of games played to decide a champion

TO LEARN MORE

AT THE LIBRARY

Clausen-Grace, Nicki, and Jeff Grace. *Basketball Science*. Mankato, Minn.: Black Rabbit Books, 2018.

Ervin, Phil. *12 Reasons to Love Basketball*. Mankato, Minn.: 12 Story Library, 2018.

Omoth, Tyler. *College Basketball's Championship*. North Mankato, Minn.: Capstone Press, 2018.

ON THE WEB

Learning more about the Final Four is as easy as 1, 2, 3.

1. Go to www.factsurfer.com.

2. Enter "Final Four" into the search box.

3. Click the "Surf" button and you will see a list of related web sites.

With factsurfer.com, finding more information is just a click away.

INDEX

The images in this book are reproduced through the courtesy of: Sportswire/ Newscom, front cover (athlete), pp. 13 (bottom), 16; Soobum Im/USA TODAY Sports/ Newscom, front cover (trophy); Lance King/ Getty, pp. 4-5; Justin Tafoya/NCAA Photos/ Getty, pp. 6, 7, 8-9; NCAA Photos/ Getty, pp. 10-11; Ben Solomon/NCAA Photos/ Getty, p. 12; Focus On Sport/ Getty, p. 13 (top); Brett Wilhelm/NCAA Photos/ Getty, pp. 14-15; Jamie Schwaberow/NCAA Photos/ Getty, p. 17; Brett Wilhelm/USA Today Sports/ Newscom, p. 20; rtrlnin764274/ Newscom, p. 21.